About the Book

Millions of years ago the earth was inhabited by huge dinosaurs—
the largest animals that ever lived on earth. Although none has
survived for us to study, their petrified footprints and bones have
been found. From them we can learn how the dinosaurs lived and
what they ate.

Like most animals alive today, dinosaurs were all different sizes.
Some ate meat, but most of them ate plants. Wilda Ross describes
these plants, what they looked like, how they grew, and where they
could be found. When the long summer of the Age of Reptiles was
over and temperatures on the earth began to vary seasonally as
they do now, the dinosaurs died off. But some of the plants they fed
upon have survived, and we can still see them and some of their
descendants today.

Wilda Ross's easy-to-read text is complemented by Elizabeth
Schmidt's colorful re-creations of the prehistoric world of the
dinosaurs.

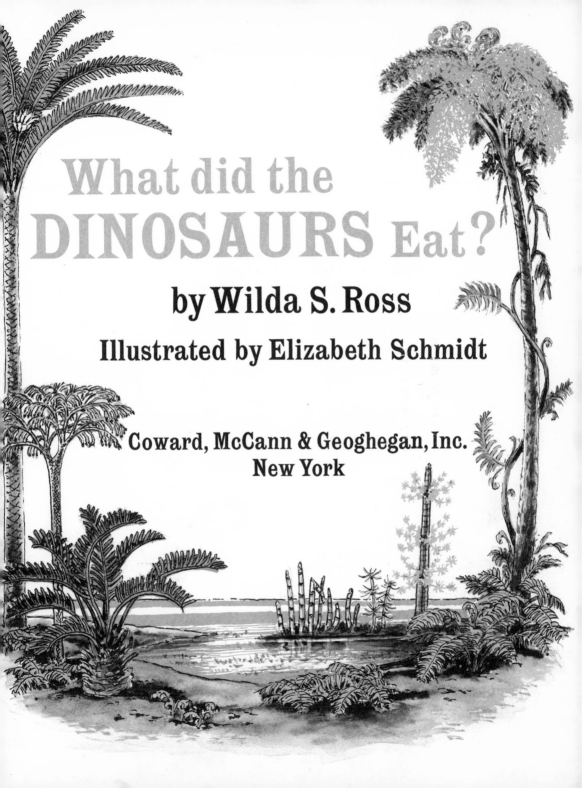

What did the DINOSAURS Eat?

by Wilda S. Ross

Illustrated by Elizabeth Schmidt

Coward, McCann & Geoghegan, Inc.
New York

General Editor: Margaret Farrington Bartlett
Consultant: Theodore D. Johnson
Montclair Public Schools

WHAT DID THE DINOSAURS EAT?

Everybody knows that dinosaurs
were the largest animals
that ever lived.
We find their bones and footprints
to prove it.
But no one ever saw a live dinosaur.
They all died millions of years ago.
Certainly they needed a lot to eat.
How can we find out how dinosaurs lived?

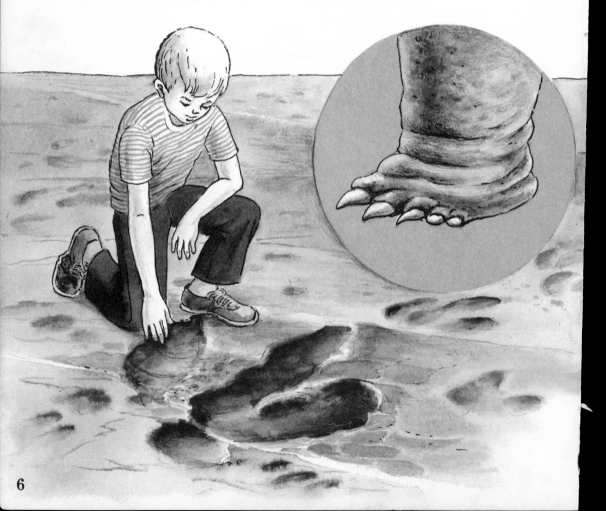

Size and shape of bones and teeth tell us the most.
Dinosaurs were all sizes,
just like animals living today.
Some ate plants and others ate meat.
The hunters or meat eaters
had strong jaws, sharp teeth,
and claws on their feet.
Like lions and wolves,
they hunted other animals for food.

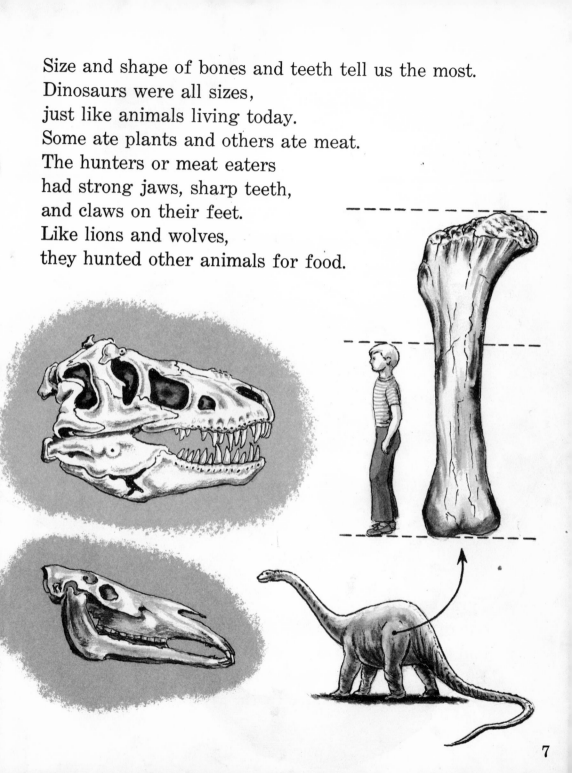

Tyrannosaurus,
one of the mightiest hunting animals that ever lived,
had a huge mouth filled with bladelike teeth.
But most dinosaurs were plant eaters.
They had flat, grinding teeth.

In our day cows and horses have flat-topped teeth
for grinding the plants they eat.
One of the largest plant-eating dinosaurs
that ever lived was Brontosaurus.

Brontosaurus waded through warm swamps and marshes,
feeding on large juicy plants.
It moved slowly
and spent a lot of time
just sunning itself on a riverbank
as alligators do.

Dinosaurs were reptiles
like many snakes and lizards, and alligators.
Reptiles depend on the sun
to warm their bodies.
Like snakes and lizards,
dinosaurs laid eggs on land.

Other kinds of animals
similar to fish, frogs, and birds
lived when dinosaurs were alive.
They were not nearly
so numerous or so large as dinosaurs.
Because the earth at that time
belonged to the dinosaurs,
it is called the Age of Reptiles.

Most of the plants
that Brontosaurus and other dinosaurs ate
were soft and juicy like pond plants.
They are called algae.
Seaweeds are algae, too.
Probably many more kinds of algae grew then.
Because they were so soft,
not many turned into fossils
to leave a record
for us to see.

A fossil is what is left of a plant or animal
that lived a long time ago.
A fossil may be a bone or a piece of wood
that has turned into stone.
It may be a leaf print on a rock
or an animal's footprint made in the mud
that hardens to stone.

Coal is a plant fossil.
A lot of coal was made
before the Age of Reptiles.
The climate was warm and moist,
and forest covered the low swampy land.
When the trees died,
they fell into the water.

Tons of mud and sand
gradually covered the mass of plants,
shutting out all the air.
Without air
the plants slowly changed into coal.
Very thin slices of coal
studied under a microscope
give us a picture of what these plants looked like.

A few living plants are
much like ones we see in fossils.
Many kinds of ferns grew along the riverbanks.
Tree ferns
like the ones we see in parks and greenhouses
were common.
They have left prints
of their delicate, feathery leaves
in the rocks.
Great masses of ferns were turned into coal.

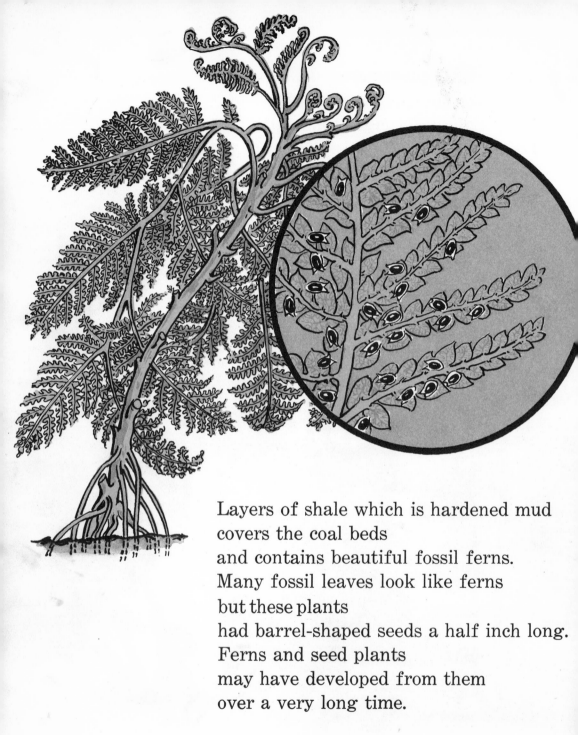

Layers of shale which is hardened mud
covers the coal beds
and contains beautiful fossil ferns.
Many fossil leaves look like ferns
but these plants
had barrel-shaped seeds a half inch long.
Ferns and seed plants
may have developed from them
over a very long time.

Ferns have small dots on the back of the leaves
that produce spores.
Some ferns have special fronds, or leaves
that produce the spores.
Spores are something like tiny seeds.
When they fall to the moist ground,
they grow into new plants.

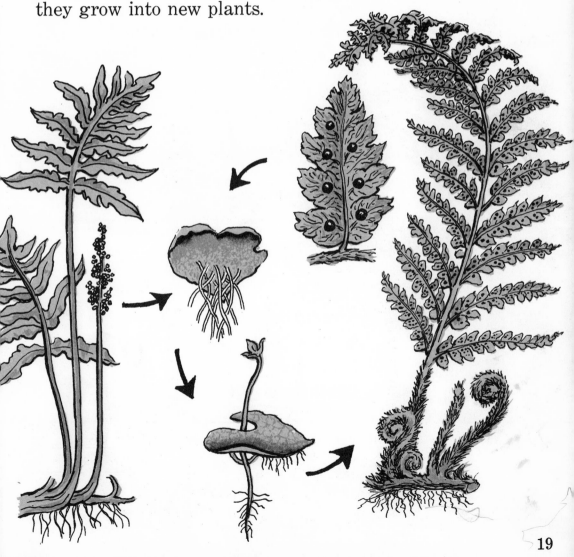

When Brontosaurus waded ashore,
it probably ate some club mosses.
Many kinds of club mosses lived then.
Some were large trees.
The few club mosses living today
are small spreading plants
that grow in damp, shady places
along with mosses and ferns.
Many people confuse them with mosses.

Club mosses are stiffer
and grow a little taller than mosses.
The stems have paired branches.
Unlike true mosses,
club mosses have roots.
Mosses have fine black hairs
that anchor them to the soil or tree trunks,
but they do not absorb water like roots.

As dinosaurs walked through the swamps
they could browse on many kinds of horsetails
growing along the banks.
Larger ones grew in the forests.

A few kinds of small horsetails
still grow along stream banks.
Their hollow, jointed stems with circles
of narrow branches look like horsetails.
But some of the stems are without branches
and have a knob like a cone at the top.
The cone contains millions of spores
which blow away with the wind,
fall onto the soil,
and become new horsetails.

These rough-feeling plants
make good pot scrubbers
because they contain sand.
Water used by the plant
contains a liquid form of sand called silica.

Cycads were common plants in dinosaurs' lives.
They grew everywhere.
Today only one kind grows in the United States,
in the southern tip of Florida.
Many cycads still live in Mexico
and other warm parts of the world.
Fossilized ones are found
as far north as Greenland and Alaska.

Cycads look like small palm trees.
The fronds, or leaves, are two or three feet long.
Stiff dark-green leaflets
grow out at right angles
from a thick center rib.
A cone similar to those on pine trees
grows at the top of the wide trunk.

A cycad might seem much too stiff and tough
for even a hungry dinosaur
with its huge appetite.
But cycads were probably once
sweet and tender.
Like all ancient plants
that still live,
cycads had to change a great deal.

When the climate was warm and wet all year,
plants had juicy, soft leaves.
As the climate became colder and drier,
many kinds of plants died.
Many dinosaurs died, too.
Those plants whose leaves gradually
became stiff and tough lived.

Certain animals
gradually learned to live away from water.
Even today a few fish
can live out of water for a while,
but they must return
to moisten their skin, breathe, and lay their eggs.

Frogs and salamanders learned to breathe on land,
but they had to lay their eggs
in water or moist places.
Dinosaurs, snakes, and lizards
learned to breathe on land
and lay their eggs on land.
They no longer had to return to the water
for part of their life.

Green algae and seaweeds
are plants that still live in water.
Freshwater algae are often tiny
and swim around constantly.
Some have swimming organs called flagella,
two of them like arms.

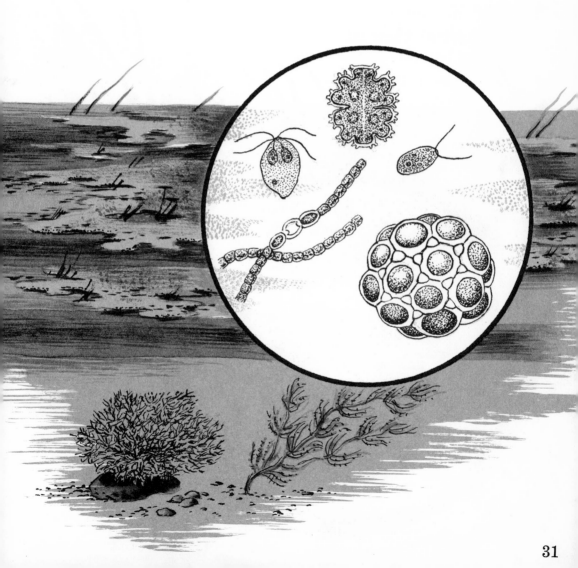

But some are leafy and attach themselves
to rocks or the bottom of a pond or ocean.
All have free moving periods during their lives
when male and female parts
break away from the parent plants
and swim about in the water
until they find each other.
Then they settle down on a rock
or the bottom of the pond
and grow into new plants.

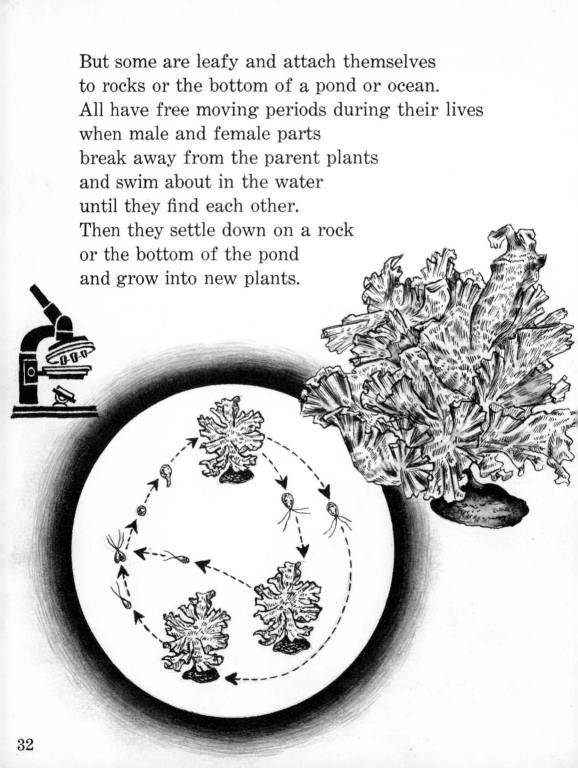

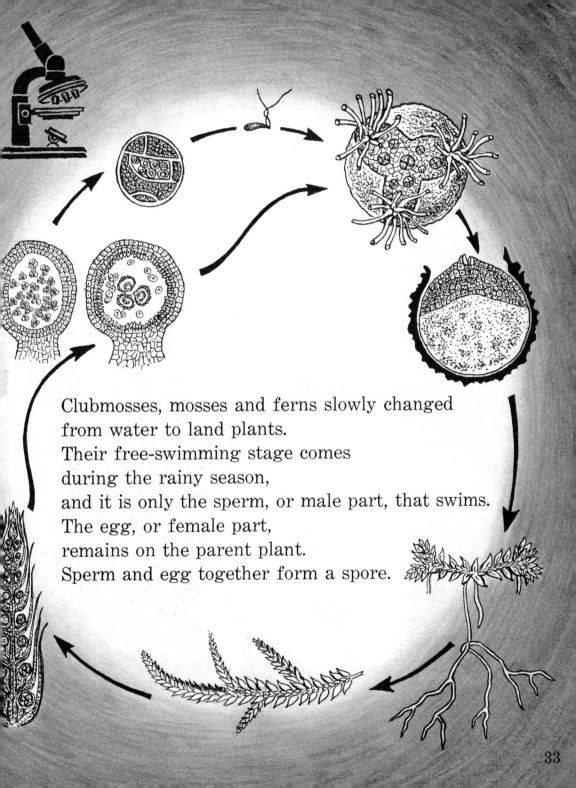

Clubmosses, mosses and ferns slowly changed
from water to land plants.
Their free-swimming stage comes
during the rainy season,
and it is only the sperm, or male part, that swims.
The egg, or female part,
remains on the parent plant.
Sperm and egg together form a spore.

With mosses,
the spores grow within a tiny sac
at the end of a long stalk
which is still attached to the parent plant.
With ferns,
they grow into the little dots, called sori,
on the back of the leaf.
Spores develop inside these sori.
When mature,
the spores fall onto moist soil
and grow into new plants.

PRESENT

TIME AFTER
DINOSAURS

TIME BEFORE DINOSAURS

Dinosaurs never had a chance
to eat grass or flowers like daisies.
These plants have seeds
and developed about 50,000,000 years
after dinosaurs had disappeared.

Each seed contains a new plant
and a small supply of food
to help the seedling grow.
Spores carry no food supply.
The seed develops inside the flower.

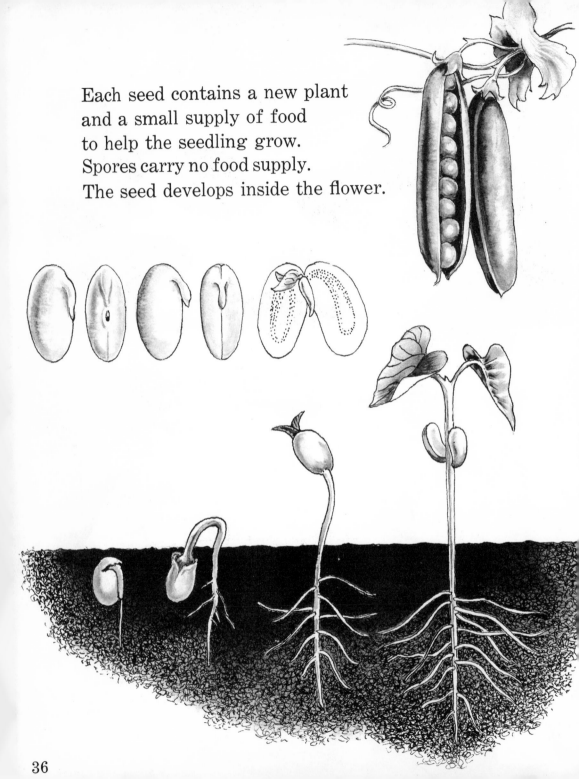

The cones of cycads and pine trees
contain seeds also.

As soon as the cone scales spread apart,
the seeds drop out.

Animals that lived during the time of dinosaurs
liked to eat pine seeds just as animals do now.

Another tree related to cycads and pines
grew in the dinosaurs' forest.
This was the gingko tree.
Many fossilized gingko leaves
are found which look like ones growing today.

Live gingko trees were first discovered
growing in gardens in China.
The leaves look like small pale-green fans
which turn yellow
and fall off as winter approaches.
The fruits look like orange cherries.

Many trees in petrified or fossil forests are conifers,
a word used for all trees with cones
such as pines, firs, cycads, and gingkos.

Tender vines grew around
the tall trunks of conifers.
With his long neck
a dinosaur like Brontosaurus
could easily have reached
into the tallest branches for these vines.

All this time the climate was changing.
Slowly and gradually the summertime world
of the dinosaurs was cooling down.
Different animals took their places.

Temperatures over much of the world
began to go up and down
just as they do now,
dividing the year
into summer, winter, spring, and fall.
Many of the swamps and lagoons
were slowly filling up
and becoming rolling uplands
covered with forests.

When plant-eating dinosaurs
like Brontosaurus died off,
meat-eating ones like Tyrannosaurus
could not find enough to eat.
So they died, too.
The Age of Reptiles was over.

The cooler parts of the earth
now belonged to warm-blooded animals.
Animals that had developed fur or feathers
and could regulate their own body heat
managed to live.
Plants like conifers with needles
or scalelike leaves
were able to withstand cold.
Seed plants could last through the winter
in the seed or resting time.

Through the years
many kinds of seed plants developed,
like grasses, berries, and fruits,
all good food for the changing animal population,
including man.
Man slowly learned to develop the plants he found
into bigger and better ones
like wheat, rice, beans, peaches, pears.
The world now belonged
to smaller animals and to seed plants.
This is the world we know today.

About the Author

Plants and animals have fascinated Wilda Ross all her life. At the University of California at Berkeley, California, she took her degree in botany. She has initiated and directed natural history programs, studied and collected ants, worked for the Bureau of Insect Identification of the U.S. Department of Agriculture, written natural history columns for the San Francisco *Examiner*, and taught classes in natural history.

Wilda Ross lives in Mill Valley, California, where she continues her interest in the study of lichens and photography.

About the Artist

Elizabeth A. Schmidt recalls that her first job was teaching art for room and board at a mission school for mountain girls in North Carolina. Her first home after marriage to Eric J. Schmidt was a yacht called *The Wave*, which was the oldest privately owned yacht under the American flag.

Mrs. Schmidt studied at the Pratt Institute and took her MA in fine arts at Wayne State University. She has been an art teacher for many years and presently teaches in San Francisco. Her work has been exhibited in many parts of the country, and she has won awards at several shows. Mrs. Schmidt and her husband live in Tiburon, California.

The *Science Is What and Why* Books

An introduction to the physical and natural sciences for the primary school child. To be read to or to read to himself. An approach planned to broaden conceptual awareness about *YOU, YOU AND YOUR EARTH* and *YOU AND YOUR UNIVERSE.*

During every active minute of his life, a child learns: through his own experiences, while exploring interests with his peers, and by communication through media and books.

Each subject in the series presents knowledge that a child can relate to his own experiences, gives information that can be examined and tested with others, and stimulates further investigation.